Unless otherwise noted, all Scripture quotations are from the International Children's Bible, New Century Version, copyright 1986, 1988 by Word Publishing, Dallas, Texas 75039. Used by permission.

Scripture quotations marked TLB are from The Living Bible, copyright 1971 by Tyndale House Publishers, Wheaton, Illinois. All rights reserved.

THE COMFORTER
© 1989 by Doris Sanford and Graci Evans
Published by Multnomah Press
Portland, Oregon 97266

Printed in the United States of America

Library of Congress Cataloging-in-Publication Data

Sanford, Doris.
    The comforter : a journey through grief / the story by Doris Sanford ; illustrations by Graci Evans.
      p. cm.
    ISBN 0-88070-331-8
    1. Consolation. 2. Bereavement—Religious aspects—Christianity.
3. Widows— Religious life. I. Evans, Graci. II. Title.
BV4908.S36 1989
248.8'6—dc20   89-39897
                                                  CIP

89 90 91 92 93 94 95 96 97 98 - 10 9 8 7 6 5 4 3 2 1

THE
Comforter

A JOURNEY THROUGH
GRIEF

for my sister Kathy . . . when you hurt, I hurt.

**The story by Doris Sanford,
Illustrations by Graci Evans**

MULTNOMAH
Portland, Oregon 97266

Dear Precious One...

If your wound is fresh, you are probably scarcely able to read just now. I remember that feeling. I wish, from the bottom of my heart, that I could infuse some of the strength I now have into your blood.

You may feel you will never heal but, dear one, you *will* heal. The good memories of the one you loved so much will stay fresh always, but this nightmare will fade. You don't have to be logical or sensible now. Abnormal reactions in abnormal times are normal.

There are kind people who will hold you up. God never intended that you make this journey alone. Please allow us to hold you. Lean hard . . . we are strong. And you have a gentle, but oh so strong Shepherd who is stronger yet. And He will carry you when your knees buckle.

No one knows exactly how you feel. Your pain is your own. But some of us have felt pain that seemed unbearable. We have made it to the other side and landed in sanity and wholeness. And so will you. Feel the pain. Share your suffering with the sensitive ones who care. It's the way God mends broken hearts. You are loved so very much by Him, and by me.

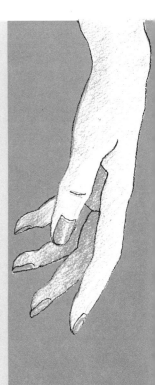

MAY 3

The two policemen wouldn't leave until I headed for the phone to call my next-door neighbor. My voice was strong and robotlike. "Janet, please come . . . they won't leave until you get here. Al is dead."

My husband had gone mountain climbing for the weekend, a favorite energy releaser after a sedentary week at the university where he was a professor. The policemen said he fell at 2:00 p.m. and died immediately. They didn't know any other details. Our children, Christy, age three, and Tim, our newborn son, were tucked in but not asleep.

Janet came right away, hugged me, and the police left. I explained the little I knew and we both stood in the kitchen numb with disbelief. She asked if I would be okay until morning. "Yes, of course," I replied. Nothing I had heard in the last half hour seemed real; it was like watching a movie. Of course I would be okay. After Janet left, I went to Christy's room and patted her until she flopped on her tummy and was asleep.

Back in the kitchen I said half out loud, "What do I do? I've never done this before. OH GOD, HELP!"

The next days came and went. I would still set the table for him without thinking, watch the clock for the time he would come home from the university, and several times I went to tell him something before I remembered he wouldn't be there. It was real, but it wasn't real.

The reality of Al's death began to soak in when I saw his body in the casket. I needed that physical proof. I was a "tower of strength" at the funeral, people said. Stoic and under control. Everyone applauded how well I was doing. In reality, I was a zombie. My state of numbness protected me from going crazy.

It was hard to sleep, and when I did, sleep was filled with violent nightmares. I wasn't hungry, but the casseroles to serve twelve continued to arrive.

I was exhausted, confused, overwhelmed, rattled, and weak. I put the toaster in the refrigerator. I couldn't make decisions. I longed for someone to take over. I remember feeling offended that life was going on in such a casual way for others. How could they go to work, mow their lawns, and play tennis? Al was dead!

The feelings came in waves. The world was turning upside down and nobody was stopping it. More and more I thought about heaven. I wanted to go there. Now. My pastor came to visit and said, "On May 3rd at 2:00 p.m., God's work for Al was perfectly, completely done. But Doris, His work for you is not done. You feel like warm Jell-O now. You are stronger than you think."

Before Al's death I had been secure, happy, and busy. Now I was going crazy.

Two weeks later, when the pastor called to invite the children and me to their home for dinner "so I could meet some other widows," I thought, *Why would I want to meet a group of old ladies?* It never hit me before that moment that I was a widow! What an ugly word.

During the next weeks and months, Janet became my rope to sanity when my emotional grip on reality was fragile—and it was much of the time. Because my parents were no longer living, my brothers and sister were on the mission field, and we had just moved to this new community close to the university, my resources in friends were limited. But Janet was there. I hadn't known her long, but her love for Jesus and her kindness to me on moving to this neighborhood had impressed me. I came to experience that the difference between emotional life and death was one person who really cared.

Talking about what had happened became one of the most important events in my life. I needed to tell my story over and over. It made it real. Mostly Janet listened, sometimes with tears, usually without comment. When she did talk she said, "I can hardly believe it myself," or, "Of course you feel rattled, Doris, anyone would. But I'll be here with you."

She knew I couldn't pray except to scream, "Oh God, help me!" I couldn't concentrate on long prayers from her either, so she shot up one-liners: "God, protect her today"; "God, please ease the nightmares"; "God, help the children stay well until she can function"; "God, help her balance the checkbook this month."

I reviewed the funeral again and again. I remembered an earlier conversation about the terrible waste of money on flowers at funerals, but I realized how much healing there was in the lavish display of love from others who also missed Al.

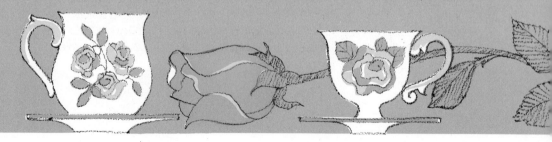

Because I was new to the church, most of the people who came to visit me were strangers. They could have said, "I don't know her very well," or, "I'm sure she wouldn't want to be bothered." Thank God, they came anyway.

And awkward nineteen-year-old students came. None of them stayed more than five minutes. They simply said, "I liked him and I'm sorry he died." Some sat on the floor and played with Christy. She missed being "roughed up" by her daddy who threw her into the air, catching her to the sound of her delighted squeals.

The brave strangers who came from church said how much they appreciated Al's dry sense of humor at the Wednesday night Bible study. They helped more than they will ever know.

It helped to have food brought in throwaway containers. It helped when others told me what they would do: "I'll be here at 9:00 a.m. to watch the children while you go to the grocery store." Many said, "Call me if there is anything I can do." But I couldn't think what needed to be done, much less initiate a call.

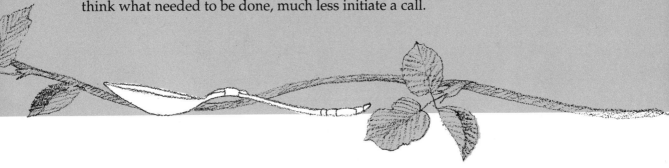

SEVEN MONTHS LATER

Reality hurt! I suffered in the beginning, but now, seven months later, I felt worse. The anesthetic of shock had worn off. Most of the supportive community from church had disappeared, believing I was "just fine now" and the work of grief was done. If I had known that I was just getting started, I'd have lost courage completely.

Sundays were terrible days. I hated sitting alone in church. For that matter, I hated the hassle of getting the children ready by myself to go anywhere. All sorts of events triggered fresh grief: hearing "our" song on the radio; driving by the university; having the car break down and the frustration of making decisions about mysterious parts which needed to be replaced; overdrawing my bank account because I forgot to enter checks. My pastor urged me to tell people what I needed and reminded me that most people don't know how it feels to be in hard grief.

Thanksgiving and Christmas were nightmares. I was incensed that I should be grateful for anything. I hated signing my name alone on the Christmas cards. And the sharp contrast of Christmas cheer with the barrenness of my own spirit was painfully clear. I went through the mechanics of the holidays on automatic pilot.

I was tempted to take the tranquilizers the doctor had given me, but I knew they would only put my grief on hold, and I would have to deal with the pain later when I stopped taking the pills. What I needed most during this time was a massive dose of hope that I would make it. Janet suggested I keep a journal of my feelings so I could see my progress.

Crying released tension for me. Janet mentioned Al's name often . . . "Al would have loved being here" . . . "That suit looks just like one Al had." It always made me cry, but she knew the tears were building up inside just waiting for permission to be released. Everything reminded me of Al and it helped to know she hadn't forgotten him and was not afraid to say his name.

Several times when we were driving I gasped as I caught a glimpse of a man who looked exactly like Al. It helped when she told me she thought he looked like Al, too. My mental health wasn't very sturdy and her observations helped me know I wasn't cracking up.

It took awhile to really understand what I had lost. One of the most "lost" elements of my marriage was being able to talk with Al about decisions. I longed to have someone tell me what to do. But friends were wise in building my confidence in making decisions and not stepping in when I asked for direction, unless I truly needed their intervention. Some helped me sort through alternatives. I was encouraged not to make any major changes for at least one year. It was good advice and protected me from myself more than once.

I found it a relief to occasionally go someplace where no one knew about my loss. I enrolled in an art class at a local community college. It felt good to step outside of my pain for a few hours each week.

I was exhausted most of the time. The demands of my new job, taking the children to and from babysitters, and continued lack of sleep left me drained. Janet's sensitive statement that grief is one of the most demanding jobs there is helped reassure my sagging spirit.

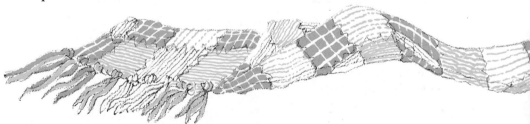

My talks with Janet about God's role in all of this had moved from the early cries for God's help to angry questions: "Why, God? Don't you care about Christy and Timmy who will never have a daddy?"

Janet never tried to speak for God and explain His actions, but quietly said, "It *is* hard to understand. God has promised to be Father to the fatherless. He knows how much you hurt and He can do for you what you cannot do for yourself. Trust Him just for the next hour. Tell Him the truth about how you feel. Say it out loud, 'I feel abandoned, God.' "

Another issue during that seven-month period was Al's clothes and his den. Having his things around didn't bother me at all, but most friends who came to the house were terribly bothered. Some volunteered to pack the things and remove them. Others merely asked *when* I was going to clean things out. The answer was, I didn't know. I would do it when I was ready. And I wasn't ready yet.

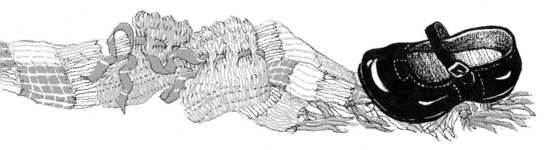

ONE YEAR LATER

The hard grief didn't stop suddenly but was beginning to fade. I was learning not to judge my level of grief by how anyone else was grieving. This was a personal journey, and it was taking much longer than most people had said it would. I was beginning to break ties to my past with Al, one at a time. My friend was right when she said, "Don't try to shut the door on the past all at once." I was learning to keep my goals small. It helped when Janet said, "Grief is not a sign of weakness. You loved Al." She encouraged me to take a break from the intensity of pain and have spots of fun. I was beginning to see that the light at the end of the tunnel was not an oncoming train! I couldn't change the past, and the only real option I had was to go forward. Like it or not.

Janet said my self-imposed pressure to "be over this" one year after Al's death was unrealistic. She encouraged me to read my journal to see how far I had come. Together we drove to the

cemetery, and while Janet waited in the car, I said an official good-bye to Al. I talked about how much I missed him and how I needed to let go of my grip on the past. This visit was a symbolic gesture. It didn't end the grief, but it did help me turn in the direction of the future.

The anniversary of Al's death was a difficult day. I went to the cemetery and burst into tears to find his grave covered with flowers from students and colleagues at the university. They remembered! That day my mailbox contained several brief, thoughtful notes: "I know today will be hard. You are loved." "I miss Al, too." "I'm praying for you especially today."

My faith had been reduced to a very primitive level that year. I had not been able to read Scripture because I couldn't concentrate. Most of my prayers were short cries for help. But what I could not do for myself, Christian women did for me. They literally carried me to God.

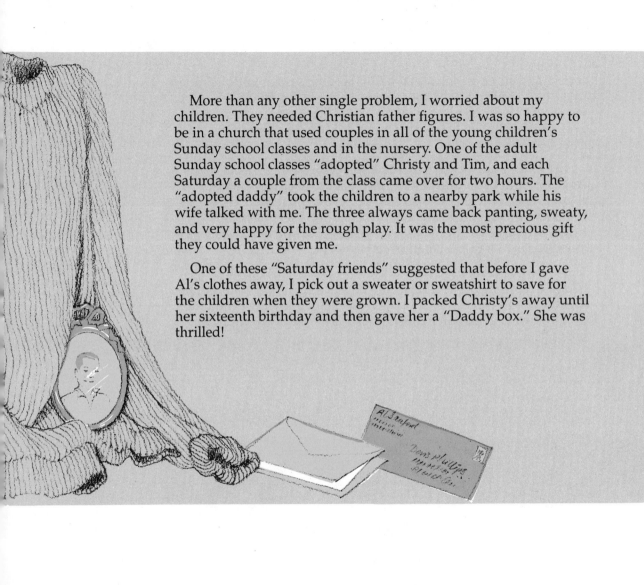

More than any other single problem, I worried about my children. They needed Christian father figures. I was so happy to be in a church that used couples in all of the young children's Sunday school classes and in the nursery. One of the adult Sunday school classes "adopted" Christy and Tim, and each Saturday a couple from the class came over for two hours. The "adopted daddy" took the children to a nearby park while his wife talked with me. The three always came back panting, sweaty, and very happy for the rough play. It was the most precious gift they could have given me.

One of these "Saturday friends" suggested that before I gave Al's clothes away, I pick out a sweater or sweatshirt to save for the children when they were grown. I packed Christy's away until her sixteenth birthday and then gave her a "Daddy box." She was thrilled!

The tears still came frequently, but not every day. When the low days came I read Al's love letters, looked at the photo album, and read our Christmas letters. The memories were precious.

Janet asked me to help her with cooking for a large dinner party she planned. It was good to be needed again. I was glad she asked.

Although it was good to be in church, I was not sure where I fit in. I didn't feel single, and I wasn't married. I decided to teach a children's Sunday school class instead of attending an adult class. Other widows have told me they were "dropped" by their couple-friends and had to start building new friendships, usually with single women.

The first year was over. I *was* stronger than I thought.

TWO YEARS LATER

I could concentrate. I could finally read all those books on grief that friends had sent me the first month after Al's death.

I was developing some sense of perspective—life was not perfect for anyone, we all have past pain, and the end of my grief did not mean I would be "back to normal." Life had changed. Our little family would never be the same. It helped to talk with other widows who said that after three years they were finally feeling strong. It was a relief to know I wasn't "weak" to have had such pain for so long a time.

The tears and sadness still came, but now they were triggered by loaded situations, such as Valentine's Day or by seeing a daddy playing with his child. Recovery didn't mean I didn't remember. It just meant closing one chapter to make way for a new one. The wounds had needed time to heal.

The "now" was not yet as good as the "used to be" but I knew that someday it would be. I was beginning to see myself as a survivor, not a victim, and occasionally there were flashes of joy and hope for a future that would be as happy as the past.

JU

12   13   14   15   16   6

19   20   21   22   23   13

My anger at the disappearance of my Christian friends was lessening. I began to understand that it was ignorance about the nature of grief, rather than a lack of caring, that led them to expect simple, immediate solutions to the complex problem of grief. Janet would smile and remind me that pain is a teacher and the lessons are learned in the furnace, not in the sanctuary. I needed to be gentle with those who hadn't had the "pain class" yet.

Her prayers for me were brief, her support practical, and her advice limited. The scriptures she shared were affirmation of God's love (John 14:18); reminders of His sovereignty (Isaiah 55:8); encouragement that He cares for the fatherless (Psalm 68:5); and the promise of our ultimate hope of being in heaven forever with our loved ones (1 Corinthians 15:23). She reminded me that God doesn't waste any experience and that I would be surprised by what God would do in my life and in the lives of my two children. It hadn't seemed possible two years ago that the promise of Jeremiah 29:11 (TLB) was for real: "For I know the plans I have for you, says the Lord. They are plans for good and not for evil, to give you a future and a hope." But the reality *was* beginning.

TWENTY YEARS LATER

Since Al's death I have talked with hundreds of new widows. Few of them needed professional help. All of them needed a friend. I've learned that pain is unique and that my experience is not prescriptive for any other woman. I've learned that grieving is as necessary in a broken relationship as it is in death.

Some losses are harder to heal than others. In general, the loss of an ambivalent or very dependent relationship heals more slowly. I've learned that time *doesn't* heal all wounds and that some wounds get infected with bitterness and self-pity. For a grief wound to heal, it must be kept clean and open to the Son. I've learned that memory can be distorted and become more black and white in time—an ordinary husband may develop qualities of sainthood he never possessed while alive.

I've learned that it may be more than this loss that needs healing. Losses accumulate and "grief overload" slows healing. I've learned that you can't choose not to grieve. If you don't let the pain out, your body will do it for you. I've learned that there isn't any right way to grieve. No agenda. No sequence. No stages. Only common feelings that are frequently a part of recovery from any loss.

In the early weeks after a loss, a woman often feels numb, stoic, insulated by shock. She looks better than she really is. She can do things she won't be able to do when the shock wears off. The reality of death hasn't hit yet.

Reality begins in about six weeks and may hit an all-time low at about six months. Feelings fluctuate on a roller coaster between depression and anger, chaos and calm. Self-worth is low. Fear is high. Friends are through listening before the widow is through talking.

Recovery doesn't come suddenly. The pain *fades*. A widow can be encouraged not to put on a mask—not to act well before she feels well. Grief recovery often takes two to three years. Acceptance of her husband's death is apparent when the widow can talk about his good and bad qualities, doesn't feel like half a person, stops running away emotionally, gets her energy back, and gradually detaches her emotional grip on the past and reinvests in someone or something in the present. Recovery means the "now" is as good as the "then." If a widow is still actively, deeply grieving two to three years after her loss, she may need professional counseling.

A caring friend can support the new widow in accepting what she cannot change; in taking care of herself physically, since grief depresses the immune system; and by encouraging the widow to keep her goals small by taking baby steps toward healing. She can be told that her need for closeness and intimacy can be met with deep friendships, but that she will need to take some risks in vulnerability. She needs to be prepared for the disappearance of couple-friends and the need to make new friendships.

A caring friend is one who knows the truth of 1 Peter 5:10 (TLB):

After you have suffered a little while, our God, who is full of kindness through Christ, will give you his eternal glory. He personally will come and pick you up, and set you firmly in place, and make you stronger than ever.

A caring friend knows that God uses pain to bring us to Himself and uses His people in the healing process.

SCRIPTURE FOR THE BROKENHEARTED

Psalm 23:4 Even if I walk through a very dark valley, I will not be afraid, because you are with me.

Psalm 34:18 The Lord is close to the brokenhearted. He saves those whose spirits have been crushed.

Jeremiah 29:11 "... I know what I have planned for you," says the Lord. "I have good plans for you. I don't plan to hurt you. I plan to give you hope and a good future."

1 Peter 5:10 ... He will make you strong. He will support you and keep you from falling. He is the God who gives all grace.

Psalm 32:8 The Lord says, "I will make you wise. I will show you where to go. I will guide you and watch over you."

John 14:18-19 I will not leave you all alone like orphans. ... Because I live, you will live, too.

Isaiah 55:8 The Lord says, "Your thoughts are not like my thoughts. Your ways are not like my ways."

Psalm 68:5 God is in his holy Temple. He is a father to orphans. He defends the widows.

1 Corinthians 15:23 ... When Christ comes again, those who belong to him will be raised to life.